Purpose for Duty and Country

ANTWAN D. SMITH

Order this book online at www.trafford.com
or email orders@trafford.com

Most Trafford titles are also available at major online book retailers.

Author Credits: I give special thanks to my three brothers Dwright,
            Dexter and Rob, my sister Joy Smith,
            my father Donnie Smith,
            and most of all, to GOD.
            For always being there for me and believing in me.

Print information available on the last page.

ISBN: 978-1-4269-6094-9 (sc)
ISBN: 978-1-4269-6095-6 (e)

Trafford rev. 04/26/2019

 www.trafford.com

North America & international
toll-free: 1 888 232 4444 (USA & Canada)
fax: 812 355 4082

"Purpose" For Duty And Country

Military life, go figure. People have been fighting wars and battles since the dawn of time. Whether it was cavemen fighting dinosaurs for food and warmth of their hide, cowboys vs. Indians for land and food, or just man's ultimate fight for survival. But these days, the stakes are a little different.

Nowadays, we fight wars and battles, simply because someone lives differently than us, these days the wars are to impose our way of life on other countries or civilizations. They don't believe in our laws and freedoms, and we don't beieve in theirs. As long as they don't try to force their way of life o us, I say live and let live. But the wars and battles are also faught for things such as oil and or gasoloine,coal, and other natural resources. As far as I'm concerned, it's all politics.

They say money makes the world go round. I'm a simple guy, if I've got something you need, and you've got something I need, we negotiate, and keep negotiating until we come to some kind of agreement or compromise.

But that's just that. These days, people would much rather fight or try and take something or get it for a little of nothing. Either way wars only lead to more wars. But that's just my take on it all. Anyway, I've been fortunate enough to talk and discuss different situations and events that took place in time of war.

I've done research and gathered information and even some of the letters being sent back and forth in times of war. And I've ran across one story in which I thought was so special, so heartfelt and unusual, that I had to share it with the world.

So with further ado, try to keep up.

Day 25

I don't know if anyone is even receiving these letters. I guess it doesn't really matter. I write to keep my mind occupied, and off of this madness. Sometimes it seems this jungle and these trees are closing in around me. My leiutenant says the trees have eyes and ears. War is no place for anybody. Life, death, who lives, who dies, I think it's all in God's hands. But I sometimes question my faith. It's not hard to do, being out here in the middle of nowhere, fighting for a reason in which you don't even understand. And when you ask questions, all you get is a response like, "that's classified." I have killed six men, three children, and a woman,all in the name of self defense. But eventually it will catch up to me. I will have to answer to a higher power. Will he forgive me? Will I suffer his wrath?

Well, to get back on the topic of thiis letter, you never know what's going to happen next. We raid them, they raid us. I wish all the killing could stop. I'm tired, this war is tired. A long dragged out fight about a little of nothing. Yesterday was not half bad. We did not run into any encounters with the enemy. Funny, we are on their land, trying to fight to tell them how they should live. Yet, we call them the enemy. We ate good yesterday, sang songs, some of us wrote letters, but for me, it was too nice a day. I just sat back and relaxed. Did alot of thinking about being back at home, prayed for my camp to be safe and for my squadron to be o.k., and tried to sleep, but come on, it's a war going on, who could sleep?

We awake this morning to gunshots sounding off about 200 yards east of our position. I can not speak or write about our whereabouts, it cold compromise our mission. We have lost radio contact with our base. And it's been twenty-five long hard days since I've felt safe. Just think 24 days ago, I was hyped up, happy, ready to go and defend my country. Little did I know, the next day I would make my first kill. I knew when I did, at that exact moment, that it would not be my last. The sarge congratulated me. Twenty years old and already I'm a trained killer.

I can hardly stay awake, but everything my eyes close, I invision the enemy about to strike and cut my throat. I even dreamed about it. I hope I make it home safe. I will make it home safe. It's time for me to go and stand watch now. I will write later. Send a return name, so I can keep writing. Bye for now.

P.F.C. Stokes
Smile, I'll make it!

Day 26

To whom this letter may concern:

I'm sorry I write you so often, but it just so happens that you live at my old address. I knew it seems crazy that I write you and don't know you, but my parents died three weeks after I graduated boot camp and I was an only child. I have no lady friend and I did not know what else to do. So it's either write you or go crazy. I chose; go crazy, but that didn't work, they didn't send me home like I planned, so I'm writing you. It's crazy, I've sent you over a dozen letters now and have gotten none from you in return., Please write back. I need you to, you are my life line. Please save my life.

My parents died in a car accident, but I feel they are still with me. My dad told me that he was proud of me and that he would always be there for me. My mom cried at my graduation. It was sad, they were so happy. That's the way i will always remember them.

That's why I write you so often. Strange as it may seems yu are the closest thing to family that I have. Please write back and tell me about yourself.l If you have a family? What type of work you do? How is the weather at home? Who won the last game between the Dallas Cowboys and the Washington Redskins? Just please write back! I feel as though I'm so alone. At mail call, all of my friends get mail, even the leiutenant gets mail sometimes. I'm the only one who hasn't had a letter since he's been here. Sometimes, I feel like giving up or i act like I don't care when I don't receive mail, but I do care, I do. It's hard and lonely enough out here.

Please write back.

P.F.C. Stokes

Day 32

Family, family, that's what I'm talking about. I can't believe it, you finally wrote back. And on top of that you called me family. Thank you so much Mr. Perkins. You have given me new life. I still can't believe you wrote.

At mail call, I was busy washing my skivies (underwear) and socks, when I heard them call my name and say that I had mail. These last few days have been hell. We've done night raids. They've attacked us numerous times. A few of my friends were killed and one was wounded and sent home. But he was so bad off, sometimes I wonder who was the luckiest, him for going home torn up, or them for dying and getting it all over with. Either way they are all luckier than I am. I'm still here, going through hell.

All my life I thought I was ready. I thought that I could handle it. Boy was I wrong. I'm scared, I'm so scared Sometimes at night, laying in the trenches, I find myself thinking about my parents being gone, and I wonder if I died, would anyone miss me. I catch a tear running down my face from time to time. Life is hard. But I will try to face it head on. I think I will be o.k.

I have to go now, but I will write more later.

P.F.C. Stokes

That Letter From Mr. Perkins

Hello son,

I truely feel as though this was meant to be. I am happy that you are calling me father. It's so good to know that you are in good health. And that everything is going fine so far. I understand that at times you are afraid. Not just for yourself, but for what you may have to do to others. And the person that you may become. But just stay grounded and focused on the person that you are now. Leave it in God's hands. He will see you through it to the end.

You have also given my life new meaning, new purpose. Thank you for that. Just think, a few short weeks ago, I was just old Mr. Perkins. A tired, lonely old man. And now I have been given new life. Now I have a son. I don't just thank God for that, I thank you. You are the bravest young man I have ever known. I mean, lots of people fight and serve their countries or what have you. But you, you stepped out on faith and faith alone. You hoped when there was no hope. You prayed when eveyone else played cards and slept. Your trusting in the Lord that he would send you a reason for being. You found me. Thank you. And if noone has ever told you this before let me be the first to say this to you. Son, I'm proud of you. If you don't give up on me, I won't give up on you.

Now that being said, we have a war to win, so let's get out there and do what we have to so you can hurry home and we can catch one of those games. Football season will be over soon but we have the rest of our lives. Focus on what's going on there and I'll handle things on this end. I love you son. Stay safe. Take care out there. And believe in God. Other than each other, he's all we've got.

Mr. Perkins
Your dad

Hello Mr. Perkins

Hello, Mr. Perkins. How's everything? Fine I hope. Things have gotten alot crazier here. I don't know how much more of this I can take. My platoon's leader is being his normal self, a jerk. But I think it's alot worse. He's gone crazy. He's starting to scare some of the other guys, but I'm trying to hold it together. It's tough.

Thanks for being there for me. You don't know how much this means to me. I've never felt closer to anybody in my life. I mean, I loved my parents and all, but you're there for me in my time of need. If anything should happen to you, I don't know what I would do. It's like you are in many ways, my father. You give me reason to want to live, to carry on, to exist. Now fighting for my country is not just a job, I'm fighting for the freedom, the rights, the lives of people that I care about. I know that at times, these letters may seem meaningless to you, but please don't stop writing. Whatever you do please don't stop writing. These letters mean the world to me. They are all that I have. You are all that I have. I will try to take some pictures of my platoon and I so I can send them to you. You don't have to put them up on your wall or anything. I just wanted you to have an idea of who you are writing and sharing your life with.

Thanks again, dad. It feels good saying that, dad. That's how I see you now. I hope it's ok with you. I can't wait until all of this is finally over and I get to come home. I hope you let me show you my gratitude. I want to go fishing with you, out to eat, and go to games. You know just spend time, family time. I'm not going to pressure you though.

So how's life on the outside? I hope you are ok. How's your health? Look, I'm going to be frank with you. I'm going to tell you just like I used to tell my real parents. Let me know what's going on with you health wise. I need to know. And let me know if you need anything. Remember, I'm family now.

I'll write you later. Thanks again.

P.F.C. Stokes
Thanks dad

Hi Dad

Hi dad,

It's me again. I just thought that I'd write you and let you know that I was thinking about you. I want to know more about you. Where you came from? What did you do? What was it like for you growing up? How old are you, dad? Any sisters or brothers? What were your parents like? Did you ever do anything in your life that you regreted or were sorry for? I want to know those things and more. It's so many questions, so many things that I'd like to talk to you about. But I guess that we have plenty of time.

What would you like to know about me? Just ask and I will give you an honest answer. It is so beautiful here. It's a shame that it's only used as a killing field. It's so nice. Look, it's their land. Dad, why are we even here? On their land, trying to tell them how to live. We can't impose our way of life on anyone else for any reason. That's not right. It's just morally not right. How did I get myself into this mess?

But listen dad, I thought that I was messed up. That is until I met this guy named James Werner. I call him Jersey, because that's where he's from, New Jersey. But he's all messed up. He had told me that he used to hustle (sell drugs) and run with a gang. But the whole time (10 yrs.), he felt like he didn't belong. He said he wanted to join the service to find his purpose. He also said that he felt as if he had found and fulfilled that purpose in joining. That he was happy here. I can't see myself being happy here. I can't see anybody being happy here. But that's just me. What do I know? I guess that you'd have to be him to understand it all.

I feel as though life is full of different people in different situations. But that's the funny thing about being in the military, people come from all over; different cities different states, and are trained to get along and lear to work together and function as one unit. That's kinda cool. But I hope that Jersey will be ok. There is this one leuitenant here who rides his ass on the regular (fuses at him about everything). I don't know why. It's almost like they are kindled spirits. They are both loners and mostly like to keep to themselves. I think that the Leui. doesn't like him because he reminds him too much of himself. They could be father and son.

The reason that I'm talking about Jersey so much is that lately, we have been standing watch together and we've been being sent on alot of missions together, watching each others' backs. And we've become friends. We are very close now. We talk to each other alot. He talks about his past and I talk about my life, mostly about you and what we'll be doing when I get home. From what he tells me, he's depressed alot. Being here, fighting the war, is his way of keeping busy and keeping his mind off of his depression. He says that he hates always being alone, feeling alone. I explained to him that I know the feeling.

And that's when I told him about you and how we met. He says that he is not crazy, that I am for pulling a stunt like that. But that he was happy because it all worked out for the best. But now me and him are like best friends, blood brothers, even. What can I do to help him. I feel bad for him, but what can I do? At times he seems to be happy, but everyone knows that it's just a front. You can look at him and see that he's hurting. Sometimes I wish that I could take the pain for him. He's only a few years older than I am, but you can look at him and tell that he's been through alot. I wonder if I could walk a mile in his shoes. It's hard being unhappy all the time, it hurts. Depression can kill a person. Noone wants to hurt all of the time. Not even Jersey. He says that he can take it. He says it makes him tougher,stronger. But I think that it is slowly killing him. I was wondering if maybe you could write him a letter to let him know that someone does care. And that God is listening. I'm sorry if I'm being out of line in asking you to do that. And I understand if you choose not to. You're already doing so much for me. I'm sorry that I even asked. Don't worry about it, just forget it. I'm sorry. I'll deal with Jersey, he's my problem. I hope that I haven't offended you.

Again, I'm sorry. I love you, dad.

P.F.C. Stokes

Son

Son,

When I read your letter, I knew where your heart was. I understood. It's ok. Everything is going to be fine. Just as i once comforted you, I will do my best to ease his pain and suffering. But it will truely be up to him. I will make an effort, nevertheless. It is no problem. I feel honored to do so. You've given me new life. For the first time in a long time, I feel as if I make a difference. Thanks son.

Now, how have you been? Is everything ok with you? I'll do my best for him, but you are my main concern. Are you eating ok? I have called around and asked if I could send you food and supplies and if so, what? And they have given me a list of things that I could send you. So I've put you a little something in this box. I hope you like it. Write me back and tell me what else you need. Please by all means, share with your friends and even with your Leiutenant if you would like. I hope it's enough. If not just write me and let me know. It's good that you have friends to help watch your back.

But you make sure that you watch theirs, also. Besides the good Lord, you guys have only got each other out there. But my son, try to pray. Try to pray alot. Not just before meals or at night. Try to form your own personal relationship with God. It will help you in life, especially out there. I know that there is alot going on out there, but stay sharp, stay focused and be strong. You will be on your way home soon enough. And I will welcome you with open arms. We will have the biggest, best dinner that you have ever eaten. Just write me and tell me what your favorite foods are. Nothing is too good for my boy. I'll be waiting on your next letter.

Dad

James or Jersey

Hi James,

Or should I call you Jersey. I would first like to tell you who I am. My name is Mr. Perkins. I'm a good friend of P.F.C. Stokes. I guess you could say more of a father. We are very close. I care alot about him, and he cares alot about you. So I guess along that vine, some where, we cross paths. Look, my boy tells me alot about you. I don't know exactly how much of it is true. But I will say this; first you are a vey brave young man for even joining the service, good job. You are ever more brave for going over there defending your country. Alot of people would have chose different. You made the right decisions, thus far. But son you don't have to be alone. You are not alone, at least not anymore. You have your platoon, my soon and now you have me routing and praying for you, also. But you ultimately have God. He's always there for you. Even when my son is long gone. Even when everyone else seems to give up on you. The good Lord will always be there with you, for you. I know that it's not easy out there. It's not easy out here, either, but we make do with what we have. Stokes said that you were a loner. That you didn't really have anybody. Noone to write or anything. And that you felt as if noone really cared. Well, I want you to know this, I care, I care about you. God cares about you. You can always write me, and I will be more than happy to write you in return. Matter of fact, write me. Write me today, as soon as you have read this letter. I will be waiting to hear from you. Tell me a little about yourself. I know very little about you. Only what Stokes tells me. I want to know from you.

And by the way, I was also in a gang, when I was younger. Give yourself a chance. Get to know me. You may find out that we have alot in common. Sometimes it seems that you are the only one on this planet that goes through life, having it hard. But you're not. And other people can relate to you because they go through it also. Just try to open up a little. You may find that this world isn't too bad a place. Anyway, watch yourself out there young man.

And don't forget to write.

Your friend always,
Mr. Perkins

P.S. Someone cares. I do.

God does. Always remember that.

Old Man Perkins

Old man Perkins,

Look old man, I know that Stokes is my boy and everything, but he had no right telling you my business like that. He should have come and asked me about me. Or if it was ok for him to tell you my shit, or even if it was ok. For him to give you permission to write me. He was wrong for that, dead wrong. But I will get at him about that later. So what you think that because you have heard a little about me that you know me now or that we are cool. Because we ain't. And you don't know me. Hell, I don't know you. Just the little that Stokes tells me about you. It's kinda cool I guess. But you see, shit like that doesn't happen to me. I'm the only one looking out for me. I have to make my own way. What works for one person doesn't necessarily works for the next person. I don't mean to come off at you like this, but please understand. I'm all that I've got, so I'm all that matters to me. I know that you and Stokes have each other now, but I've learned to rely souly on me. I'm used to depending only on me. And if I let myself get sidetracked by anything or anybody, there's no telling what could happen. I have to keep my edge, especially out here. Out here, where noone can hear you scream. I have to stay focused. So I hope you don't take this letter the wrong way, but all it takes is for me to be daydreaming one day about being back home or about a letter that you or someone else wrote me,anyone else. And in the blink of an eye, I'm dead. So I'd appreciate it if you'd stop writing and trying to pry. Believe me, I am grateful, but you have to understand my position. You take care of yourself old man.

P.S. Thanks again, but no thanks.

James Werner
"Jersey"

Hi Dad

Hi dad,

I'm sorry for the way Jersey acted. I just heard about that letter that he wrote you. When I asked him about it, he snapped on me. He literally went crazy. We must have argued for hours. I was trying to let him know that I was just concerned about him. That I was trying to help. It's hard out here anyway, but being out here by yourself and having noone to talk to, noone to write and nothing to look forward to is plain old insane. But Jersey pulls it off well. I don't know how, but he does. He's followed up by saying that his life was his business and that I should leave him alone and stay the hell out of his business and mind my own. I think that in a sense, he was right. But I also think that he understood what I was doing and that he appreciated it. So I'm apologizing for him and for myself for butting into his business in the first place.

Still though, I can't help but notice him bieng on edge lately. This war is doing something to him. I mean everybody is tense, but Jersey is a little too tense. He's ready to shoot anything that moves. And he has no conscious. I asked him the other day, how did he feel about all the people that he and I have had to kill so far? I also said that one day some how, some way, we would both have to attone for what we've done. We would be held responsible for our actions, and how he felt about that? He just said, "whatever happens, happens." And he looked away, as if to try not to think about it anymore.

I just left it at that. I thought that everything was everything, but then last night I kinda overheard him crying to himself. It wasn't the first I've caught him doing it, either. I hope he's ok. I don't know how to come out and ask him what's wrong. What should I do? What should I say? I mean you don't know how hard it is. Dude has been there for me. He has saved my life on more than on occasion. It's almost like, nothing scares him, nothing bothers him. And nothing affects him. How do I deal with someone in that state of mind. I've actually watched him kill someone with his bare hands, washed his hands, and about 15 minutes later, he is sound asleep. Only to awake in the middle of the night and listen to him sniffle and whimper for about two hours. He need me. But how can I be there for him?

I've often asked my Leiutenant, but he says just give Jersey time and when he's ready, he will talk to me. What do I do until then? Earlier tonight, we heard gunfire not too far away from our position. But the Leiu. called it in and said for us not to worry our other battalion was in the area and had it all under control.

I'm scared dad, I'm so scared, for all of us. Why did this war had to happen? Why did we have to be here? Wars don't change things, they just postpone and prolong them. But how long can we do this? How long can this war last? I guess that I will find out soon enough. So anyway how have you been? Do you need anything? Let me know. You're there for me dad, let me be there for you. I hope everything is going well. You know what, I can't wait to get back home and see that old house. I'll bet you have made plenty of changes and repairs to it. And more than anything, I can't wait to come home to you. Pop, thanks for everything. These few months have gone by so fast it's unbelievable. Soon I'll be there and I can take care of you for a change because you've done so much for me. It's not as hard out here, knowing that I have someone on my corner backing me. Thanks again, dad.

P.F.C. Stokes

Dad

Dad,

How are things back at the house? Fine I hope. I know that I just wrote you yesterday, but I didn't know what else to do. Dad I don't know how else to say this, but Jersey's dead. Dad, I don't know know what happened or what went wrong. Last night he seemed to be normal. At least normal for him. He talked alittle, he even listened for awhile. He smiled a time or two. And he even told one or two of the old stories about where he's from. He called it nowhere. But later on, at lights out, I listened for him. You know, to see if he was crying again, but he wasn't. Matter of fact, all I heard was paper crackling softly. And it sounded like he was whispering to someone. But I didn't think much of it. I just tried to sleep, as hard as that would be, out there. But when we awakened this morning, Jersey was gone. Poof, without a trace. We were all puzzled for a long while. What happened to Jersey? Did he desert us? Did the enemy get to him? Was he dead or still alive? We had plenty of questions, but no answers.

Anyway, after a short while, parties. We went out in groups of three. One tracker, one weapons specialist, and one marksman to each party. It was a weird feeling, but we all kinda knew that Jersey was dead. What we didn't know was how did the enemy get pass our duty watcher. And why did they just get Jersey, where did they take him? We would all have our answers soon enough.

The search went on for hours. I had just finished my search for him, when I went into my little ditch, sleep area. I hadn't even noticed, but there was a letter. At first, I thought it was from one of the other guys, or from the Leiu., or something say that they are sorry for what had happened, because everyone knew that Jersey and I were really close. But then, as I was tearing into the letter, I remembered tat noone knew exactly what happened yet. So the letter couldn't be from them. And I also remembered overhearing Jersey last night crackling paper. That's when I knew that it must be from Jersey. And all of the commotion, I didn't see the letter at first because I wasn't looking for it. I was looking for my friend, my bro, I was looking for Jersey. I opened the letter and read it. It terrified me, dad. In the letter, Jersey had said that he was sorry for us arguing about me asking you to write him. He also said that he loved me, that I was the closest thing he had ever had to a brother. He said that he always wanted to protect me because I was his only family. Dad I can't stop crying. He said that I was the only one in this messed up world that he trusted. He went on to say that he owed me his life, time and time again. He said for me to tell you thanks for everything. He said to tell you that maybe in another life you also could have been friends, family even. He said that you would understand. Dad, then he said that he could not take this anymore. The loneliness, the quiet, the fighting, the pain. Dad he said that this would be his last time ever speaking to me or anyone else. That he was going into the jungle, away from camp, and end it all. He said that he love me and he was sorry that he was leaving me by myself, but that I still had you. He said that it was something that he had to do. He said to smile and remember that he would always be watching over me, waiting for me to come and join him in the here after. He asked me not to tell anyone of his plan. That he would make it look like they got him. He also gave me readiness on how to reach the place which would be his final resting ground. Dad, when we found the body, he had been shot in the head and was also hanging from a vine, by the neck. Was he hanging himself when they found him and shot him. Did he climb the tree, place the vine arond his neck and shoot himself? Dad, my biggest question is... do I keep his secret? And how do I not tell anyone? Dad I'm so scared. I feel so alone. Why did Jersey do that, why? I don't know what to think. I don't know what to do.

P.F.C. Stokes

Twelve days since receiving Stokes' letter

Son,

Listen to me, this is your dad. I know that I'm not your biological father, but I'm still your dad, just the same. I know you're scared and that you're sad. But now is not the time to lose it. You have to be strong right now. For you, for me, for your squadron. God will see us through this. We just have to be strong and have patience. There are going to be hard days, easy days, sad days, and so forth. But we have to keep the faith and stay focused. I'm sorry for what happened to Jersey, but I'll be damned if I'm going to let it happen to you. You will be ok, you will make it. And I'll be waiting right her for you. We will make it together. We both tried to reach out to Jersey. I guess that we didn't do it soon enough. It was already too late for Jersey. He was already gone. It's not your fault what happened to him.

And about him asking you not to say anything to anybody... what do you think? That's a demon for you to battle alone. I can only give you my opinion. If it were me, I think that Jersey cared for you enough that he felt like he abandoned you. He felt like he owed you an explanation. He wanted to help bring closure to all of your questions. I know that he only raised more questions, but at least he tried. He trusted you, he loved you, you. So it's up to you on what your decision will be. I know it's not an easy onel. But I want you to know that I stand behind you 100% on whatever you decide to do. I'm In your corner.

Son, I'm sorry it took me so long to write you back, but I've been under the weather a little. I'm feeling better now, though. This damn cold. I'm not going to burden you with my problems. I'll be ok. You just make sure that you be ok. I'll write you again in a few days.

Dad

Dad

Dad,

How have you been feeling lately. I know that in your last letter, you said you had been under the weather. But also that you have been feeling better. I hope and pray that everything is ok. Dad I sent you a money order. I hope that you are not mad at me for that. But I know that you're not as young as I am, and money is sometimes hard to come by for us all. Bills don't pay themselves. And think of all of the care packages and things that you have sent me. It's just a little something to say thanks for everything, dad. I wish that I were there now, to cook for you, or maybe even clean the house so you can get off of your feet and sit back and relax, or just to be there, for you. Thanks for your last letter. I needed that. I needed to know that someone heard me, that someone cared. I know that what happened with Jersey wasn't really my fault, but still I can't help but feel like I may have push him too hard, to fast. But I was just trying to help, dad. I miss Jersey so much. With his "don't give a damn" attitude. It's been quiet for the past few days, a little too quiet. I guess that God was just having a moment of silence for Jersey, my brother.

Dad the air around here is starting to stink of blood and death, when it used to smell so rich and pure, so fresh. This war will be over soon. I can feel it in my heart. One way or another this war will have to end very soon. It's a nice day out today, so I'm going to try and enjoy some of itl. I'll write you later.

Love you, dad.

Stokes

Son

Son,

Hello, how are you. I was just cleaning out the attic a few hours ago. I'd never been up in the attic until last week. I had a few things to put away and decided to go and check my attic to see how much space I had in there. I saw a few old boxes up there. Well, I didn't look into them then, but today I did. I found so many interesting things. I found all kinds of old photo albums, old clothes, and keepsakes, things of that nature. At first, I was not sure if they were things that your family left behind or what. But then, I noticed at the back of the album, it had your family name on it. So I knew then that they were your family's things. I hope you don't mind me looking into them. But, I did learn alot more about you and your family history. You have a beautiful family. I'm sorry, you had a beautiful family. You look just like your father in these pictures. I wish that I could have known you back then. You look so happy. I know that your parents would have been proud of the man that you've become, because I am. I felt so warm and happy, looking at the photos. But seeing them, I was also indifferent as to how you would react to my pictures. Yes, I said to myself that I would send you a few of your family's keepsakes and also a few pictures of you guys. But also, that I would have an idea of who we were actually talking to and writing to. And also have a greater understanding as to why God chose us to be there for one another. I hope that you are o.k. with the pictures and all.

Take care, I willl write you later.

Dad

Stokes

Stokes,

Son, I know it's not easy. Seeing as how we are of different race and origin. But any way you slice it. I love you. I'm here for you. And I will continue to be here for you when you need me. Color doesn't matter. As far as I'm concerned, I'm still your father and you are still my son. You are just confused right now. But don't worry, I will give you time and space to gather you thoughts. You are one of the best things to ever happen to me. Don't lose sight of thatl. And I will do whatever is in my power not to let it all slip away. We need each other. We are all that we have. Every since my seeing those pictures, I've hoped and prayed that God would see us through all the madness of race, color, and sinicism. But, I can see now that it will take some of us a little longer than others.

I will pray to God again tonight that he help you to come to terms. But whatever you decide, I will respect your wishes. I pray that one day we will again be able to call each other family. I will end this letter in saying: son, I love you.

Mr. Perkins

P.S. Think of all we had, all we have been through together. Son, don't let it all go to waste. I will give you time to think. I'll be waiting to hear from you.

Mr. Perkins

Mr. Perkins,

I'm sorry. I don't know why this has affected me like this, but it has. I wish that things were different. Why did yu have to be, well you know. And why does it hurt so bad to know? I don't know what to say. I don't know what to do? Why did we get so wrapped up in each other? Why? What, did God play a stupid joke on us both? Well, I don't get it. I guess that the joke is on me. I hate you, and I hate myself for hating you. But it doesn't change anything. I still hate you. While we were busy writing each other, I don't know why none of this ever came out. Look, thanks for everything that you have done for me, and for being there for me. I'm sorry that it had to be this way, but it's complicated. I can't take it. It's enough to have to fight this war, but to have to deal with this also, too much. I'm sorry, I never would have written if I'd have known. Through it all, neither of us never thought to ask that question, as if it didn't matter.

Ha! Now I see what Jersey meant when he said that I was only asking for trouble. What was his philosophy? "Let the world worry about the world, take care of yourself. What's right here, right now. Everything, everybody else doesn't matter. The minute they do, you're dead."

Please dont take this the wrong way, but, I'll be o.k. from here on in. Don't write me anymore and this will be my last letter to you. You helped me through some hard times, but now I don't know if it was worth it all.

You take care of yourself old man. Another place, another time maybe, but not here, not now.

P.F.C. Stokes

P.S. I did learn something in it all! I wasn't going to write you this letter, but you earned it, you deserved it and I needed to. I'll miss you old man. You did teach me to care, to love, and how to be a man. A man would of written you and bring closure to this all. So I did.

Mr. Perkins

Hello sir,

You don't know me, but my name is Sgt. Mills, Richard Mills. I'm one of Stokes' Sgts. in the division. I know that we don't know each other, but I think what you did was a kind and noble act; if I have ever seen one. You did what not many people would have ever done. Stokes told alot of us of the whoe incident. And then to find out that you are not of the same place, you still insisted on carrying on as if it didn't matter. Stokes was ashamed of it all. I told him that he should be ashamed of himself. I don't know if it means anything to you, but I would have been proud to call you dad.

I will say what Stokes is afraid to. Thanks, for me and him. You don't know how much you not only meant to him, but to alot of us out here. We would all sit back and eat some of the goods from your care packages, and read some of your letters. You are the best thing to happen to quite a few of us out here. We all got together and told Stokes that he was being selfish, childish even. And we told him to grow up. He know that he still cares and loves you. How much you two meant to each other. That doesn't just go away over night. Stokes even admitted so himself. He misses you alot. He came to me today and asked me to write you, that he was afraid because of how he acted in his last letter. He still loves you, Mr. Perkins, alot. And not only him. You have alot of us up here caring and being more compassionate toward one another. We are, alot of us are of different race and even different religion. But seeing as to how you and Stokes came across each other and became family, you have given alot of us new hope.

So for me, writing you was not a problem. As a matter of fact it's my honor. I'd like to have a part in mending you two's relationship back together. A part in history. Because we all said that this would go down in history, that we would tell our kids of this story. And our kids' kids.

Thanks for everything.

Sgt. Mills

P.S. You can always write me, I'll write you back, friend.

Sgt. Mills

Hello,

First off, thank you. I needed a letter of that calliber. I really neeed to hear these kind words of encouragement. I know that it's hard for you guys out there, believe me. But, it's also hard for us folk back home. I mean it wasn't exactly hard for me to accept the fact that Stokes and I are of different race. But what was hard, was breaking the news to him. I never wanted to hurt him. I love Stokes as if he were my own blood and even more so. I don't know what to do to be honest. But what I do know is that I can't be the one to write that first letter. Stokes has some healing to do. Healing and growing. Acceptance is the key. So maybe with a little bit of prayer, and some talk from guys like you, he will come around.

Thank you again Mills, for everything. And he doesn't even know it, but my health has gotten worse. I have a bad heart. I wasn't going to tell him until he came home. I didn't want him side-tracked or worrying about me. He has enough to worry about out there in that field. I'm glad that you wrote. I haven't heard from my son in weeks.

Yeah, please let him know that I still see him as my son. Just a little confused. So it's good that you wrote and let me know how he was doing. I was getting pretty lonely and worried. Please feel free to drop me a letter anytime. If there's a problem, something I can help you with, or just to talk. And I will be honored to return a letter to you. You've helped more than you know. Hopefully, I will hear from my son soon. I miss him so much.

Mr. Perkins
Friends always. Thank you.

Mr. Perkins

I'm sorry. I'm sorry for everything. I started writing you. You didn't ask for any of this. It was pushed on you, by me. You accepted, and took chance. You were there for me when no one else was. You had me covered. And I thanked you by pulling a stunt like that.

Mr. Perkins, you have to believe that I truely am sorry. I've been talking to alot of the other guys here. From the Leiutenant to the Sarge to some of the other privates. And they all said the same thing, that I acted like a jerk. I mean, I still care for you alot. And I really do miss you. But it will be hard for me to call you dad. At least for now. So please continue to write me and be there for me. I have alot of growing up to do. I hope you willl be around to help and watch me grow.

But Mr. Perkins, I never lied to you. As hard as it was at time to discuss and admit. How I felt about everything, I never lied to you. Deep down inside I still feel as if you're my dad. It's like before you became a part of my life, being out here was one big nightmare. But since we've known each other, everything is a little easier to cope with. Even the hardest of times some how seemed easier. Thanks.

But calling you Mr. Perkins just doesn't feel right. We're family. Not because we had to be, but because we chose to be. And writing this letter right here, right now, I realize that you have always been and will continue to be my dad. I'm sorry, dad. Please forgive me. Please write me back. I know that I hurt you. I hurt myself. I will end this letter in saying please forgive me, please continue to be my dad. And reguardless of your decision, I will always love you.

P.F.C. Stokes
Your Son

P.F.C Stokes

So son, where do we go from here? I don't know what to say or how to feel, as you would put it. Our lives have been very interesting thus far. I love you, son. Truely I do, but how do I know that you won't change up in me again in the future? What guarantees do I have that you will love me unconditionally? When I chose to return that first letter, it didn't matter what color, race, or creed you were. I just knew that you needed something, someone in your life to help you to understand yourself as well as what yur purpose was. You needed to know that you made a difference.

And son, you still do. I have loved you since that first letter, and I still do. Maybe we both moved too fast, maybe not. But the question still remains. Where do we go from here? I will always be here for you We are family. God saw to that. Are you still praaying? Asking forgiveness for your sins? I know that I am. We all fall short for the glory.

Son, the other nnight I had a dream. I dreamed that you did not make it home to me. I dreamed that you finally got back, came home from the war, and you let something as petty as this take you away from me. Son, please don't ever reject me again. Come home to me. Give an old, dying man his last request. One wish, that I could sit and talk with my son, not of natural birth, but that was a gift from God.

Remember son, I will always love you.

P.S. Write back soon.

Still your dad,
Mr. Perkins

That Day. That Damned Day.

It was just another night. The end of a long day. Mr. Perkins hadn't heard anything from Stokes in about two weeks. But it didn't bother him because he knew that they had been under heavy attack lately. And that a few of his new found family members had be killed. He had been praying for them all. He had been receiving letters from so many new people since that one day, so long ago. He was happy, oh so happy. But none was as close to him as his new-found son. He missed Stokes and their letters greatly.

Where was his son?

Was anything wrong?

Had anything happened to him?

—————————————————

Old man Perkins chose not to think of things like that, but still he could not help but worry. That was his son. By chance they had crossed paths, but through faith and love they became father and son. And in a way in which no two people had ever loved each other more.

So coming back to the present day, about a week earlier, Mr. Perkins had sent out quite a few care packets. Some to a few of his new friends, and newly adopted family, and even one to stubborn ass Leiutenant Flowers. Now again with a name like Flowers, why the hell was he so damned crazy. His name should have been Thorn maybe or Briar Bush, but not Flowers.

But none of the care packets together could touch the one he sent to his boy. Cakes, chips, skivies(underpants), socks, t-shirts, and even magazines and books. Playing cards, I miss you cards, puzzle books, extra paper and writing utensils, toilet paper, and everything. Nothing was too good for his boy.

The box was so big, so heavy that it took two people to carry it. But of course, being the person that he was, he would share with the people who had little or nothing. But the old man's questions remained... had he received his package?

Was he o.k.?

Why hadn't he heard from his boy?

So, the next morning, Mr. Perkins called down to the base nearest to his home and started to ask questions. But all they said to him is that they were sorry, but that they could not help him. That it was all classified. They could not disclose the location of where Stokes and his platoon had been sent. That it would compromise the mission. But they did tell him that he would be notified as soon as they were able to notify the families, which could be days, weeks, or months.

What to do, what to do. An unhappy Mr. Perkins sat and waited, and he waited. But in the military, no news is good news. About three days later Mr. Perkins does his usual morning routine. Brushes his teeth, wahes up, and puts on his robe to go and check the mailbox. Again, it was empty.

But this particular morning about eleven thirty, he receives a knock at the door. It's Col. and two captains. One has a flag, the other an envelope. He knows then that his boy is dead. He immediately falls to his knees and asks the Lord... Why?

Why did my boy have to die?

'Why didn't you send him home to me?

I have noone left Lord, I have nothing. He was all I had. The Col. talked with Mr. Perkins and had listened to the story of how he and Stokes had became father and son. They read over alot of the letters from Stokes as well as some of the others. They even ran across a letter from Lt. Flowers, thanking Mr. Perkins for all he had done for him, Stokes, and the rest of the whoe platoon. It brought tears to all four of the men's eyes, but it was a good cry. The Col. had never heard of a story such as the one Mr. Perkins had told him. And to top it all, Mr. Perkins had the letters to back the stories. It ws truely a miracle how it all happened.

A few days later, was the funeral. The Col. came as well as Mr. Perkins and had the families of the other fallen soldiers. Every one thanked Mr. Perkins for what he had done for their sons, uncles, brothers, and a few of the young men who passed were even fathers. The Col. notified his superiors of the whole situation/ incident. And soon the word had spread about it all It was even on television, about how a young brave soldier unknowningly started a movement by simply sending a letter to a person that he never even met, asking for compassion, companionship, and how the letter came to the perfect soul, Mr. Perkns. A few short weeks later Mr. Perkins received a medal of commendation and for duties above, beyond, and never ever done before, for the first time in recorded history a civilian was awarded the purple heart. Where he read what would be his son's final letter. Which reads as follows:

Hi dad, I know you haven't heard from me much lately, but we've been under heavy fire. But even through all the shooting, running, hiding, and killing, I've been thinking about what you said about giving myself to God. I even went to the platoon's so called chaplin, I call him P.K. (preacher's kid), his father is a Reverend. Anyway, I had him Baptize me as best he knew how and he did. I've also been praying to God asking him to forgive me for all of my sins against Him, against man and animal Mike. I miss you dad. I hope that you are proud of me. I should have written you earlier. And believe that I would have if I could. It's funny I've never even seen or talked to you in person or on the phone, yet and still, I think about you all the time. Even more so than my own parents. You're what gets me through these hard times. Don't worry dad the Good Lord will bring me home soon. Hold on Dad, we are taking on enemy fire. I have to go now. They're coming. I'll write you later.

I love you.

Mr. Perkins goes on to say that must have been when it happened. my son's last words were that he loved me, me. And that he would be home soon. Mr. Perkins then paused for a minute and stumbled, almost as if to fall over.

Holding his chest, he then looks up to God and realizes that God did send Stokes home. To his true home and that it was also his time to return home.

To the ashes from which he once came.

On that day, Mr. Perkins died on that platform knowing that he would see his son for the first time, on the other side.

"Purpose" For Duty and Country
by Antwan Smith

Printed in the United States
By Bookmasters